Octopuses, Squid, & Cuttlefish

Contents

- About Cephalopods 2
- Octopuses 4
- Squid 10
- Cuttlefish 16
- Fascinating Creatures! 22
- Glossary 24
- Index 24

Text by Stanley L. Swartz
Photography by Robert Yin

DOMINIE PRESS
Pearson Learning Group

About Cephalopods

Octopuses have eight arms. Squid and cuttlefish have eight arms and two tentacles. They belong to a group called **cephalopods**. They live in the ocean.

◀ Cuttlefish

Octopuses

An octopus can be very small or very large. It hides in caves. An octopus can change colors when excited. This helps it to hide from **enemies**.

◄ Octopus

An octopus eats fish, crabs, and shrimp. It uses **suckers** on its arms to catch prey. Suckers are also used for crawling and swimming.

◄ Octopus

This octopus lives near a **coral reef**. One octopus can lay more than 50,000 eggs. The eggs hatch in four to eight weeks.

◀ Octopus

Squid

Squid have two **tentacles**. These are longer than their arms. Tentacles are used for touch and taste.

◀ Squid

Squid are fast swimmers. They can dart backward when scared. Squid squirt ink to escape from **predators**.

◀ Squid

Some squid are **luminous**. They have light-emitting organs in their bodies. The lights help squid see other squid.

◀ Luminous Squid

Cuttlefish

Cuttlefish are related to squid. They also have tentacles. Tentacles are used to capture **prey**. The tentacles can be drawn into pouches.

◀ Cuttlefish

The cuttlefish's body is wide and flat. Cuttlefish have strong **jaws** for chewing food. They live in very deep water.

◀ **Cuttlefish**

Cuttlefish have an **internal** bone.
Their bones often wash up on the beach.
Some people collect these bones.

◀ **Cuttlefish with Diver**

Fascinating Creatures!

Octopuses, squid, and cuttlefish are fascinating creatures! They can be kept in **aquariums** as pets. Some people catch them in the ocean and eat them.

◀ Cuttlefish

Glossary

aquariums:	Glass tanks used to hold marine life
cephalopods:	Marine animals with large heads, large eyes, and tentacles
coral reef:	A hard shelf of coral
enemies:	People or things that threaten to hurt you
internal:	Inside something, such as an animal's body
jaws:	The part of the mouth used to bite and chew
luminous:	Something that is bright and glowing; filled with light
predator:	An animal that hunts and kills other animals
prey:	Animals that are hunted, caught, and eaten by other animals
suckers:	Organs that are used to attach an animal to an object or a surface
tentacles:	The part of the mouth used to feel

Index

aquariums, 23
arms, 3, 7, 11
cephalopods, 3
coral reef, 9
crabs, 7

eggs, 9
fish, 7
ink, 13

jaws, 19
ocean, 3, 23
predators, 13
prey, 7, 17

shrimp, 7
suckers, 7
tentacles, 3, 11, 17